Contents

New words

cross
(verb)

different

famous

heavy

jump
(verb)

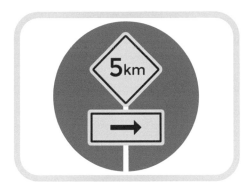

kilometre
(noun)

place
(noun)

strong

valley
(noun)

visit
(verb)

What
is a bridge?

Bridges go from one **place** to a **different** place. People **cross** bridges in cars, buses and trains. They can walk on them, too.

This bridge crosses a river.

This bridge crosses a **valley**.

Djurdjevica Tara
Bridge, Montenegro

Millau Viaduct,
France

THINK!

Is there a bridge near your home?

7

How long are bridges?

Some bridges are very long. This bridge is for trains – it is 165 **kilometres** long!

165 kilometres

This bridge is for cars and buses – it is 55 kilometres long.

Bang Na Expressway, Thailand

People walk on this long bridge.

Charles Kuonen Suspension Bridge, Switzerland

Danyang-Kunshan Grand Bridge, China

FIND OUT!

Use books or the internet to find out how long the Charles Kuonen Suspension Bridge is.

Are bridges strong?

Some bridges are very **strong**. Cars, buses and trains are **heavy** but they can cross bridges.

This is a strong bridge.

The New River Gorge Bridge, USA

Tilikum Crossing, USA

LOOK!

Look at the pages.
Are the bridges safe, do you think? Why?

How do we make bridges?

We make strong bridges with stone and metal.

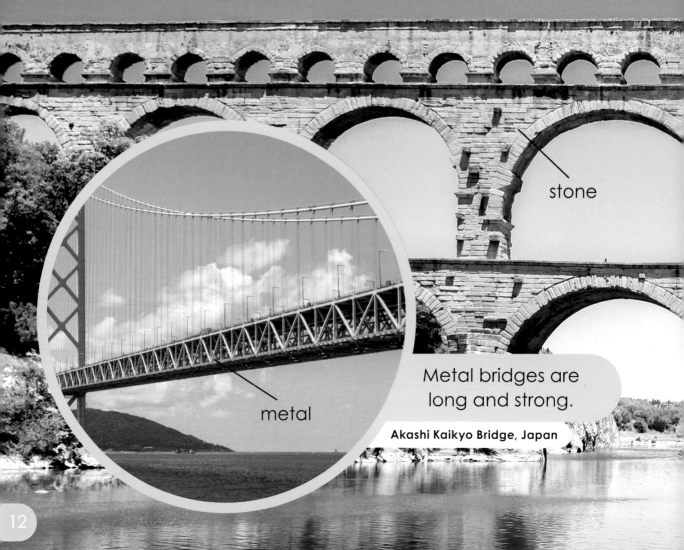

Pont du Gard, France

stone

metal

Metal bridges are long and strong.

Akashi Kaikyo Bridge, Japan

We make bridges with wood, too.

wood

Rope can make a strong bridge.

Q'iswa Chaka, Peru

rope

FIND OUT!

Use books or the internet to find out about Inca rope bridges.

Are there different bridges?

There are many different bridges. Beam bridges and arch bridges are old.

Rakotz Bridge, Germany

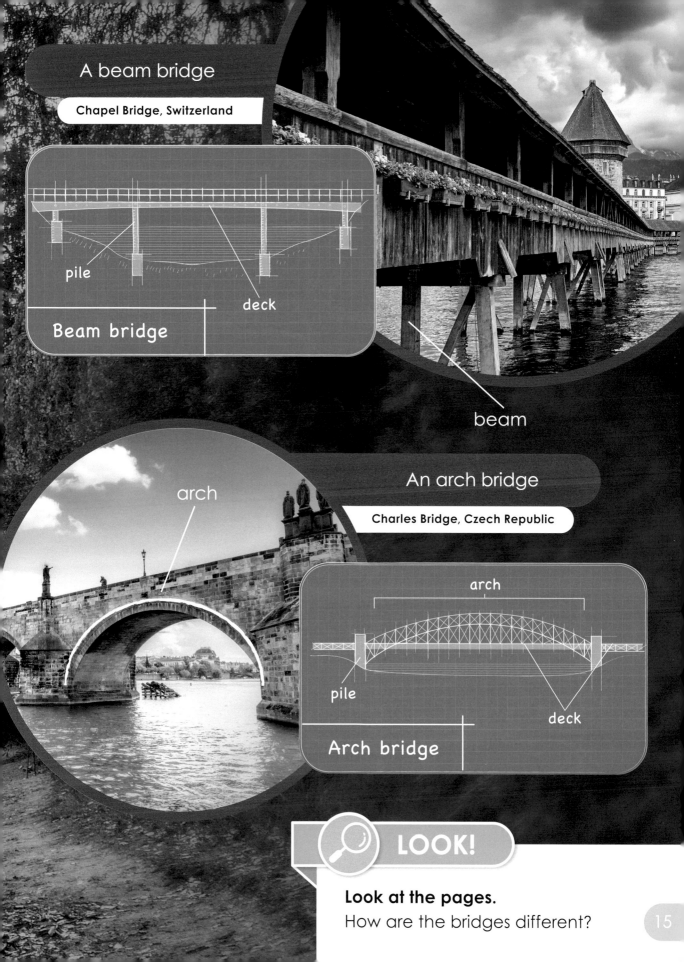

A beam bridge

Chapel Bridge, Switzerland

Beam bridge

pile

deck

beam

An arch bridge

Charles Bridge, Czech Republic

arch

arch

pile

deck

Arch bridge

LOOK!

Look at the pages.
How are the bridges different?

15

Today, we have metal cantilever bridges and suspension bridges.

suspension

Rio–Antirrio Bridge, Greece

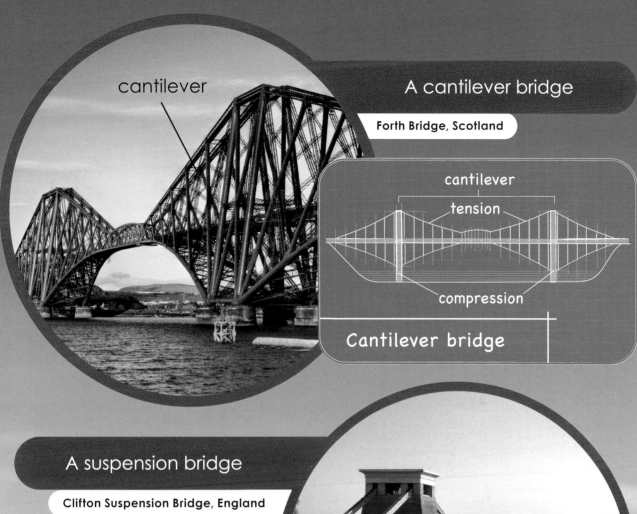

cantilever

A cantilever bridge

Forth Bridge, Scotland

cantilever

tension

compression

Cantilever bridge

A suspension bridge

Clifton Suspension Bridge, England

pylon   suspender

Suspension bridge

🔍 LOOK!

Look at the pages.
Draw the different bridges.

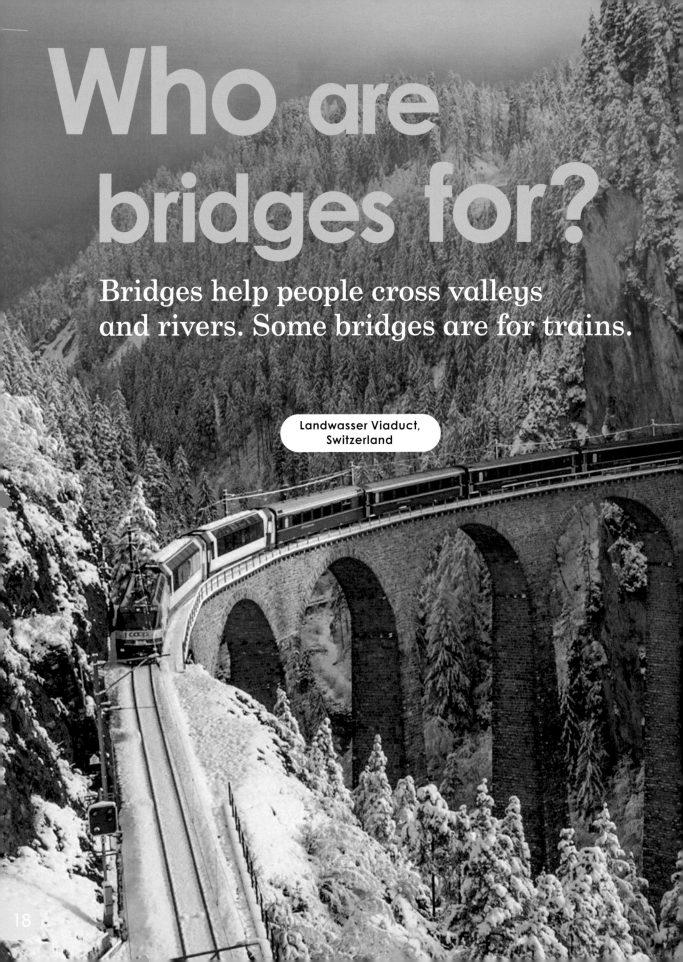

Who are bridges for?

Bridges help people cross valleys and rivers. Some bridges are for trains.

Landwasser Viaduct, Switzerland

People walk on this bridge.

Millennium Bridge, England

Tower Bridge is for cars, buses and people. It crosses the River Thames in London.

Tower Bridge, England

▶ WATCH!

Watch the video (see page 32).
How do boats go under Tower Bridge?

Do animals use bridges?

People use bridges, but some animals use bridges, too! People make bridges for animals. This bridge crosses a road.

Dwingelderveld National Park, Netherlands

monkey

This bridge is for monkeys.

Monkey Corridor, Brazil

leaf

ant

These ants make a bridge. They cross from leaf to leaf.

FIND OUT!

Use books or the internet to find out about more animal bridges.

Are there any new bridges?

This glass suspension bridge is new. Walk on the bridge and look at your feet. You can see the trees under the bridge!

Zhangjiajie Glass Bridge, China

glass

This new bridge crosses a river.

Tbilisi Bridge, Georgia

Boats can go under this new bridge.

Gateshead Millennium Bridge, England

PROJECT

Work with a friend.
Make a poster about the Gateshead Millennium Bridge. Draw pictures on your poster. Show how boats go under the bridge.

23

What are some famous bridges?

The Golden Gate Bridge is very **famous**. It is a suspension bridge. Many people **visit** it.

Golden Gate Bridge, USA

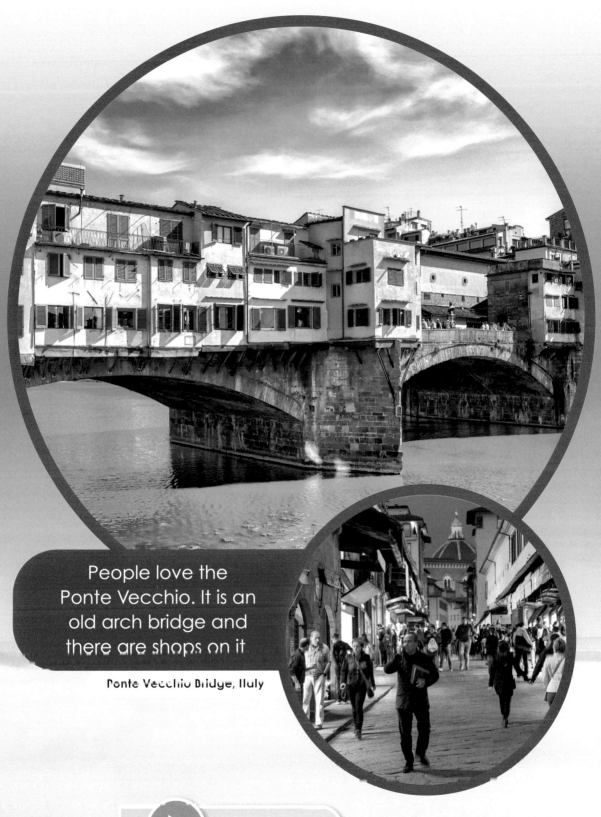

People love the Ponte Vecchio. It is an old arch bridge and there are shops on it

Ponte Vecchio Bridge, Italy

WATCH!

Watch the video (see page 32).

Do you recognize any of these famous bridges?

What can you do on a bridge?

People can enjoy bridges.
Some people use bridges for sports.

This person is **jumping** from a bridge.

Kawarau Bridge, New Zealand

steps

Can you see the people on this bridge? It has 1,332 steps. At the top of the bridge, you can see the city.

Sydney Harbour Bridge, Australia

PROJECT

Work with a friend.
Find out more about bungee jumping.
Do you want to try? Why?/Why not?

People walk on this bridge. They look at the beautiful mountains and trees.

Golden Bridge, Vietnam

People sit on this bridge and talk with their friends.

Khaju Bridge, Iran

mountain

clouds

Look at this bridge. Walk on it and you are in the clouds!

Langkawi Sky Bridge, Malaysia

THINK!

Look at the bridges in this book.
Which bridge is your favourite?
Draw a picture of your favourite bridge.

Quiz

Choose the correct answers.

1 Bridges can cross . . .
  a rivers and valleys.
  b buses and trains.

2 People . . . on
this bridge.
  a walk
  b drive

3 We can make
bridges from . . .
  a river.
  b wood.

4 Beam and arch
   bridges are . . .
   a new.
   b old.

5 This bridge is for . . .
   a monkeys.
   b elephants.

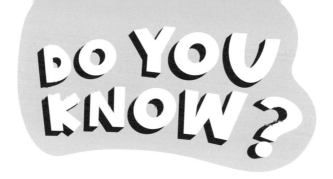

DO YOU KNOW?

Visit www.ladybirdeducation.co.uk for
FREE **DO YOU KNOW?** teaching resources.

- video clips with simplified voiceover and subtitles
- video and comprehension activities
- class projects and lesson plans
- audio recording of every book
- digital version of every book
- full answer keys

To access video clips, audio tracks and digital books:

1 Go to **www.ladybirdeducation.co.uk**
2 Click 'Unlock book'
3 Enter the code below

kwFBzCBUIm

Stay safe online! Some of the DO YOU KNOW? activities ask children to do extra research online. Remember:

- ensure an adult is supervising;
- use established search engines such as Google or Kiddle;
- children should never share personal details, such as name, home or school address, telephone number or photos.